MW00626121

this SPECIAL LIFE

Living with special needs
& LOVING it.

RHIANNA SANFORD

Table of Contents

Dedication

This book is dedicated to every mama who loves a child with special needs, and to those children who make our lives an inspiration to the world.

Foreword

I can completely relate with Rhianna Sanford's experience with "This Special Life!" First as a former pediatrician, I cared for many children with special needs and always had a great love for them. But I never understood "This Special Life" until God blessed our family with our second son, Mark Andrew Hunsley. When he was eight months old, he had a seizure that lasted four hours. By 18 months, we received the diagnosis of Dravet Syndrome, a rare genetic seizure disorder, and by the time he was two, we got a second diagnosis of Autism. For the first time in our lives, my wife Kay and I actually understood what it meant to be parents of a child with special needs! We felt the immense stress, the stares when we went out in public, and even experienced the grief of losing those dreams that we had for Mark.

Due to what I have learned from Mark, God allowed me to become a Children's Pastor at a large church in Kansas City for five years. God then led me to Grace Church in Overland Park, Kansas, where I started the SOAR (Special, Opportunities, Abilities, and Relationships) Special Needs Ministry and am now the SOAR Special Needs Pastor.

On November 1, 2010, Mark was cured of his Dravet Syndrome and Autism when he was born into Heaven at the age of five and a half. The only way we are able to cope and make it day to day is through the love of our Lord, Jesus Christ, and we firmly believe in the biblical truths that Rhianna shares in this book. Kay and I were blessed to be Mark's parents! He never did belong to us. He belonged to God and was on loan to us. God used Mark's time here on earth with us to teach us and prepare us to be able to minister now to hundreds of other families and to walk alongside with them, through the highs and the lows. It is easy to always look for all of the negatives that are happening in our lives, but I want to encourage you to change your perspective and see how you really are being blessed! Our children are a gift from God. They are created in the image and likeness of God. They are NOT a mistake! I would do anything to observe Mark having another seizure, or another autistic meltdown; but, I take complete comfort in knowing that this was all part of God's plan, that Mark is now in Heaven, with a completely perfect body, no more seizures and able to talk in full sentences!

Because Mark is in Heaven, and because God blessed my family with him, today I am passionate for families with special needs and work endlessly to minister to them, which fills me with complete joy. I am living out Mark's purpose! SOAR Special Needs Ministry is Mark's legacy and purpose. As of August 2017, SOAR currently ministers to over 650 individuals with special needs of all ages and severities and we have also assisted over 150 churches from all over the country in starting or improving their special needs ministries. Because of Mark, God has given us the vision to help develop 1000 special needs ministries in churches throughout the world in the next 20 years! In much the same way, this book is one of the purposes and legacies of Kaiya for her mother, Rhianna!

This is a book that EVERY parent of a child with special needs must read. While it may be written more towards mothers and from a mother's perspective, trust me, as a father, it applies to us dads as well!!! Dads, this is one of the best things you can do for your family. Grab this book. Read it and apply it! It really does make a difference. These truths can change your outlook from despair to hope! Have I had days that I struggled and was mad with God? Absolutely! Is that okay? Absolutely! Are we supposed to stay in that mindset? Absolutely NOT! This book will help give you practical guidance in changing your mindset!

Rhianna has learned what it truly means to live a "special life." Her daughter, Kaiya, is a complete blessing who can speak volumes without uttering a single word! In the following pages, you will meet someone very much like yourself, a parent of a child with special needs, who has her own struggles every single day. Even so, she has made a conscious decision, which has changed her entire outlook and allows her to overcome adversity. My prayer today is that you read this book with an open mind and an open heart, and allow yourself to really hear the heart of Rhianna and what she is sharing with you. God bless you, Rhianna, for listening to God and sharing these biblical truths to help parents of children with special needs realize that they were actually created for "This Special Life!"

Doc Hunsley
SOAR Special Needs Pastor
Grace Church
Overland Park, Kansas

Introduction

Everyone knows what it feels like to experience something completely and totally unexpected. No matter who you are, I can assume that you have been smacked in the face with a reality that has completely caught you off guard and left you in utter cluelessness. Like seriously— CLUELESS! So what does a mother do when she is suddenly rocked to her core and told that her kid may never walk…or talk? What does a father do when he has to wonder if he will ever get to play that quintessential game of catch with his son? How do you continue to live with the same heightened level of hope and excitement as before?

Life, as well as its turn of events, to a parent of a "special needs" child, is indeed unique.

It is by far, one of the most challenging circumstances. Simply put...IT. IS. HARD. One of the reasons it is so challenging is because it is in most cases very UNEXPECTED. "Yeah! I want a kid with special needs when I grow up!" said no one ever. Who would ever desire even a hint of *negativity* in their parenting role? The greater impact, however, is that it generally means that life will be DIFFERENT from the lives of most of the people you know. Therefore, you feel alone. You feel secluded. You are quite sure that no one else REALLY understands what you are going through. And honestly, some of us parents of special needs children might feel like we've been let down somehow.

Look. This book's purpose is not to answer the question of why your child is the way he/she is. This book is purely purposed to help you realize and walk out the actualization that in spite of the condition of your child, your life can still be pretty spectacular. I need you to believe that! If that feels like an impossible idea to believe currently, please, KEEP READING! Why? Why do I need you to believe that something, which may have brought you pain, despair, embarrassment, or even anger, can actually be the reason why your life can still be incredibly awesome? It's simple. This "special" life is inclusive of your "special" child. No matter what issues and diagnoses your child may have, they need you at your best. They need you to live your BEST life. They need the person YOU ARE MEANT to be, regardless of his/her disability. You will not live your BEST life if you are consumed with sorrow, anger, or guilt over why your child is not like other kids.

Several years ago, I came face to face with this serious urgency to upgrade my perception of my life as a mom of a special needs child. My very sanity as a mom to my little one was hinging on welcoming a new picture of how my life could be. It has been a process, but with God's help and divine wisdom, I have come to a place where I can actually embrace this life and all that comes with it! Even in the craziest and messiest of moments, I have a broad sense of gratitude.

In this book, I will share three Biblical truths I have learned that have led me to this enlightened, peaceful place. These truths, when applied to your life, will enable you to navigate the extraordinary territories of your "special" life and equip you to excel at living, no matter the circumstances surrounding the needs of your child. They ultimately will help you to look at life with new eyes and be assured that you were created for this. Additionally, they will help you with the difficult moments that come in this kind of life. As you continue reading, I pray it will lead you to become the divinely, empowered mother your child needs you to be. Are you ready to truly LIVE your "special" life?

Chapter One

What is Normal Anyway?

When you've been thrust into the land of the "special," you can respond in one of two ways. You can, of course, throw yourself a pity party and grow bitter over the fact that your life is different, or, you can embrace the life you've been given and transcend even your own expectations of how amazing life can be. You can absolutely adore your life! Your life IS different. But, who says that "different" is bad? Why do we automatically assume that just because one thing is uniquely different from another, that it must be worse? My husband, someone who is the epitome of one who embraces his particular uniqueness, professes that each one of us has the opportunity in life to create our own "normal." Your normal may not look like my normal and that is perfectly okay. In fact, that's the way it SHOULD be! A preconceived idea of a "normal life" mostly results in a life of major disappointment. That preconceived idea leads to a belief that life is **supposed** to be a certain way. Then, when our lives don't look like what life is **supposed** to look like, we feel gypped or like we are somehow victims. Oh yes. I have been there, Friend. Then, there is the danger of comparing your life to someone else's. You know how it is when you look at your friend and covet her non-therapy ridden calendar, non-wheel-chair pushing, and non-overgrown, diaper-changing life. While it is normal, comparing yourself to others is terribly toxic to your emotional health as a special needs mama.

There is a standard, however, for you to measure your life, which is the Word of God. It is indeed the "blueprint" to use in all of life's seasons. Only God knows the beginning from the end. He alone has the playbook of life with all the winning plays for YOU in YOUR LIFE. Just because we have lives that look different from most others we know, does not mean that we are discounted from receiving the same godly promises laid out in His Word! Your life is just that, YOUR LIFE, given to you by God. It is unique to you. No one can live out your exact purpose and reason for existence other than you! Isn't that exciting? No matter what happens in your life, which was given to you by the ultimate Creator of all things, be confident that you already have what it takes to be able to embrace, enjoy and excel in what was created just for you.

"His divine power has <u>given us</u> <u>everything</u> we need for a godly life through our <u>knowledge of him</u> who called us by his own glory and goodness." 2 Peter 1:3 NIV

My husband is right. We absolutely do get to choose what our "normal" is. And really, it doesn't matter what we face. That verse above says that we can have *everything* we need to live a "godly life." Now which would you prefer, a "normal" life or a "godly life;" a life full of mediocrity or a life full of divine power; a life that is good or a life that is GREAT; a life that looks like everyone else's or the life <u>YOU</u> were meant to live?

Most of us plan to do the "normal" things. We plan to go to college. We plan to get married and have cute babies some day. Most of us plan to get a nice, grown-up job that will pay the bills and provide for our families. This is the "American Dream," right? As a young girl, I watched my mother climb the ladder of great success in corporate America and just knew that I would follow in her footsteps. After all, we had nearly the exact same skill set! I was strong in the administrative field as she was. I spoke intelligently as she did. I, like her, worked well with others and was a team player while also displaying the qualities of a valuable leader. I had even learned from her the significance of dressing a certain way to display my professionalism. So, I THOUGHT I had it made. I was going to climb that ladder just like she did and make a lot of cash. *Just.*

Like. Her. But, what if ... just, what if, the way my mother succeeded in life is NOT the way I was to succeed? What if God had something altogether different in store for me?

Well, as I am sure many special needs parents already know, it is extremely difficult to do the corporate America thing when there are multiple therapy appointments, doctors' appointments and even hospital stays that are a part of your "normal." When this became a reality to me, suddenly, my life was just that...mine, and no one else's. I had to stop looking at what other people's lives were like and start embracing what was unfolding in front of me. More importantly, the habit of seeing myself as anyone other than who God created me, Rhianna Lynnise Sanford, to be was going to lead to complete dissatisfaction. Speaking from experience, that is a very depressing place to be. This leads me to the first biblical truth for any parent in my shoes to do if they want to embrace and love this life: *Accept that your identity is in God, through Christ, and not in man.*

Chapter Two

Truth #1: Your Identity Is In Christ, Not In Man

I had to realize that I was not supposed to live a life that looked just like my mother's simply because I AM NOT MY MOTHER. What God has called me to isn't better or worse than that of my mother. It is merely unique to me. Knowing your identity is crucially linked to the acceptance of your contrasting life. Your life may not look like your best friend's life, your father's life, your sister's life or anyone else's life at all! You have your very own thing to do. You are particularly unique and NO one compares to YOU. God has placed such a specific plan and road in this crazy world for you to travel on. And guess what? It is NOT ONLY to be your special child's parent! Yes, that surely is a big part of it! But, if I were **only** to be a mother to my child, could I also be an author and write this book? Could I also be a business owner and contribute to the financial needs of my family? Could I also be a vocalist who loves to be used by God in the area of worship ministry? If I allowed the circumstances of my life limit me from doing <u>all</u> of what God has designed me to do, I would be SO BORED, not to mention, unhappy. People are not fulfilled in their lives many times because they are not living THEIR LIVES! Many of us have made the decision that big goals and/or achievements must be left to those who have "normal" children. NO WAY! You may have your hands full, but the dreams and desires God put inside you still matter! Living your very specific life and carrying out what you were always meant to do, leads to an exciting, fulfilling life. Anything less casts a dim light on life and feeds ongoing frustration.

For we are <u>God's handiwork, created in Christ Jesus</u> to do good works, which God prepared in advance for us to do." - **Ephesians 2:10 NIV**

There is a divine anointing in you to live this special life well.
Believe it. From the very moment of your conception, God had "good works" for you to do. He had a dream for you to discover and one day realize.

The "specialness" in your life does NOT have the power to disqualify your dreams.

Your identity rooted in Christ means that you get to be only who HE says you are, no matter what. When you know that, I mean really know it deep down in your innards, you see life with such elation! You become aware of great purpose and your mind is alive to all kinds of opportunities and experiences. Finding that enlightening perspective brings fulfillment for your very existence on this earth and is flat out priceless. This connection to God's plan for your life creates a protective shield of joyful bliss that preserves you from the toxicity of comparing your life to others. The fear of "missing out" on what is "normal" becomes obsolete.

You find yourself comparing the abilities and experiences of other children, less. And the anger towards whatever diagnosis connected to your child disappears. You hold your head up as an overcoming victor, rather than, an overwhelmed victim. You start to realize that this life is less about what you THOUGHT it was "supposed to be like" and more about the supreme plan of God for YOU and YOUR FAMILY.

There is something so empowering about knowing who you are and knowing what you were created to do! For me, this is the foundational truth, which allowed me to begin to embrace this "SPECIAL" life. More importantly, once I was able to correctly identify myself and embrace that identity, I was then able to correctly identify my precious, special needs child. This leads me to what may be an uncomfortable question for you. How do you identify your special needs child? Do you see her as a victim? Do you see him as a child that wasn't given the same attention in the womb as other children? I remember well the heartache I felt as I looked at my daughter and then compared her to another child her age who could do so much more than sit in a wheelchair and watch the other kids run, jump and freely interact with one another. Your child is just as valuable to God as those "normal" children. He has a unique, God-given purpose. Wholly believing this very much removes the harshness of whatever disability or limitation your child may have.

If you can cling to the truth that no matter what, your child can do whatever it is his Creator created him to do, it becomes so much easier to look at your child with joy in your heart instead of grief. When it comes to your child's purpose on this earth, there is no disability. The earlier mentioned verse, Ephesians 2:10, absolutely applies to your "SPECIAL" child as well! God has created something magnificent for your child to do! It may not look like that of other kids. Guess what? That's completely okay! Virtually, what really matters is that your child can sense that you are fully and completely in love with who she is. When you look at her, can she see your adoration of her, or does she see your pain? Does he sense that you believe in him to complete his unique calling, or does he sense that you feel like you are missing out on something? Good or bad, your energy can have substantial effects on your child's overall well being.

As important as it is for you to know your own identity, it may be even more significant to know your child's identity. Special needs children are still God's creation, fearfully and wonderfully made. They are these amazing creatures with divine purpose and power to affect the world in their own matchless way! I don't know about you, but that thoroughly excites me! I feel especially honored to be the parent of my kiddo! This enlightening perspective of how you see or identify your child is incredibly empowering. For me, it has totally disarmed me from constantly fighting with a preconceived idea of who my child was SUPPOSED to be. Ohhh...the mental battles I have fought! Today, I look at her, freely smiling with adoration and look forward to the things we will experience together as God continues to creatively work in her and in me.

This foundational truth is so pivotal that I have created a space for you to honestly reflect for a moment. First, think about how you have seen or identified yourself up to this point in your life. Then, write that down in the space provided. Next, write how God's Word describes you. On the following page, there is room for you to do the same with your child. First, write how you identify your child, then, write down how God's Word identifies him/her. (For assistance, see index for scriptures on identity.)

I cannot express enough how important it is for you to be completely truthful and transparent with yourself. The more honest you can be, the more liberating and transformational this activity can be!

Reflections

1.   How have I identified myself?

_____

_____

_____

_____

_____

_____

_____

_____

_____

2.   How does God identify me?

_____

_____

_____

_____

_____

_____

_____

_____

_____

_____

_____

_____

_____

_____

3.   How have I identified my child?

_____

_____

_____

_____

_____

_____

_____

_____

_____

_____

_____

4.   How does God identify my child?

_____

_____

_____

_____

_____

_____

_____

_____

_____

_____

_____

_____

_____

_____

Chapter Three

God's Truth is a Luxury

We tried for six months to become pregnant with our first child. We were so excited to start a family to pass on the immense love we had for each other. I don't know if there is a more exciting idea to a young couple who are so crazy in love, than the idea of having a child together to share in nurturing and raising. There were lots of preconceived ideas about the kind of things we would do and experience as parents. We knew we needed to be on the same page about how we would discipline our child. We wanted our child to be connected to both of us so we had planned that my husband would get up at night to bottle-feed breast milk so she'd have that sense that she needed her papa too, not just her mama. When we found out that we were having a girl, I had visions of dresses and bows and of her dad being so protective of her going out on dates one day. I prayed that one day we would be as close as I was with my mother and enjoy shopping and singing with each other as we rode together in the car. There were so many things we THOUGHT we would experience with our baby girl.

When our daughter, Kaiya, was born, she was the most angelic thing we'd ever seen. Words cannot describe how doll-like she was. She was perfect. She would develop normally over the next several months, smiling, laughing, sleeping through the night, sitting up on her own and even start to utter "mama," "papa" and "ink" for drink. Little did we know that those would be the only words we'd hear her say. Around the age of nine months, Kaiya started to "go backward." She was slowly beginning to lose her fine-motor skills and had become very clumsy with her toys and cups. We were scratching our heads as her parents but her doctor was telling us there was nothing to be concerned about. We had never been parents before, so we thought maybe this was normal. By the time she turned a year old, we KNEW something was indeed, not normal. Her words had completely disappeared and she wasn't even trying to crawl. Something was not right. Fast-forward through two and a half years and the thousands of miles we traveled to see various specialists who would order numerous assessments and more blood work than a little girl should ever have to endure. This seemingly endless search for answers was our normal for almost three years! Why was our sweet baby girl who seemed so perfect, not perfectly "normal"? When she was three and a half, we had finally gotten an answer. She was diagnosed with an incurable, neurological disorder called *Rett Syndrome*. We were told that she may never walk or talk and would probably need everything done for her for the rest of her life. While that was not the most desirable of news to hear regarding this angel that we altogether adored, my husband and I were more relieved to finally have an answer, than depressed over what that answer meant. Please follow me closely over the next few sentences. Rett Syndrome was the diagnosis and we were living in the reality of what that meant. But because we knew and understood that both our identities and hers are directly connected to a divine and purposeful plan, we were not immediately filled with insurmountable fear. The truth of who we, as a family, were in God's eyes, was more powerful than any fear that tried to control us as to how she would spend the rest of her days on this earth. Am I saying that I have never had a weak moment? ABSOLUTELY NOT! There have been many tears and hard moments. But over the years, I have made a conscious decision that no matter what we face, in the end, God made me a winner and He also made my daughter a winner so, why act like I've lost something?

Knowing your identity awards you with the luxury of divine truth. To further comprehend that, let me define what a luxury is. A luxury is a pleasure that is out of the ordinary. In other words, it is something that is enjoyed, though, unexpected to be experienced by most. The biblical truth of "No weapon formed against you shall prosper," (Isaiah 54:17), belongs to you if you identify yourself as a child of God. Therefore, you can take pleasure in those things that may be undesirable or out of the ordinary because you know that you will not be defeated. The truth of "God is working all things out for the good of those who love the Lord and are called according to His purpose" (Romans 8:28), is for you to take advantage of because no circumstance can overthrow God's supreme will for your life. Knowing your identity in Christ gives you the same power of Christ to overcome. Knowing that "we have NOT been given a spirit of fear but of power, of love and a sound mind" (2 Timothy 1:7), is a luxury in the midst of the most frightening of situations! Living in divine truth regardless of the circumstances creates a spirit of peace that is so far-reaching, that the human mind cannot comprehend. I have lived through some very difficult moments and experiences, as my gorgeous daughter is now a teenager. But, through every trial, God's Word, the True Word, the Living Word, has been our weapon to fight against overwhelming fear and depression in this life that I never expected I'd be living. I know that I can take God at His words of truth because I am His beloved child and fully comprehend that He made me to be more than a conqueror, through His love.

"No, despite all these things, overwhelming victory is ours through Christ, who loved us."
Romans 8:37 NLT

Your identity is someone that has been granted the luxury of God's Word that is applicable to any situation you may face. Without God's Word being buried in our hearts and minds, we would have felt what I'm sure most parents feel when they are told that their child whom they've had so many exciting imaginations for wouldn't do the same kinds of things that "normal" children do: despair, fear, anger, unbearable pain, grief, etc. Going through life and all of its surprising twists and turns without knowing that you were created to live your life based on the truths of the Bible, is like going to war with nothing but a spoon. Life is full of battles, big and small. Regardless of the battles, you WILL WIN THE WAR. Using God's Word to fight your battles doesn't mean that everything will be perfect. Though, it does mean that instead of feeling defeated, you will have hope and faith that you will come out on the winning side in the end. WHY is that? Because you are God's! Because you're a co-laborer with Christ! And because God has already graced you with what you need to be victorious!

Chapter Four

Truth #2: the GRACE factor

Her lips were blue. Though the natural color of her lips is a blushing pink, over the course of these particular 45 seconds, her lips had turned blue. Her sweet, yet, frail, three-year-old body was uncontrollably convulsing and seizing for the hundredth time over the course of a few days. They just kept coming to the point that she couldn't hold her head up, nor swallow the smallest bite of food. Then, the seizures got longer and longer, robbing her lungs of adequate amounts of oxygen. To say this would be a nightmare, for a mother and father to watch their baby girl as oxygen left her body, is an understatement. And yet, neither one of them felt fear. Neither one felt doubt. Lastly, neither one even shed a tear as the blue lips of their little angel continued to appear.

Why didn't we panic? Why didn't I scream out in fear for her life? There's no other way to describe it, other than there was a tangible presence that literally maintained our composure on our behalf. The human, fleshly part of our beings, was pushed to the background. And the spiritual, God-like part of our beings that only saw the TRUTH within the present situation was in total control. This divine, spiritual influence, I speak of, is called *grace.*

What is GRACE?
Many believe grace is only favor from God, which is undeserved, yet freely given.

Especially in the environment of the church, we hear this word in that context a great deal. It is many times paired with the same meaning as mercy, as it is used below.

"In Him we have redemption through His blood, the forgiveness of His trespasses, according to His riches of grace" - **Ephesians 1:7 NIV**

Clearly, the meaning of grace above revolves around us receiving something from God even if we didn't ask for it, and even if we don't deserve it. I'm quite grateful for grace described in that way! However, as I've lived this uncharted life and experienced God's divine power to excel amidst the challenges, I've found grace to be something other than unmerited favor.

Paul's familiar testimony of the "thorn in my flesh" is a great example of how grace also operates.

"Therefore, in order to keep me from becoming conceited, I was given a thorn in my flesh, a messenger of Satan, to torment me. Three times I pleaded with the Lord to take it away from me. But he said to me, 'My grace is sufficient for you, for my power is made perfect in weakness.' Therefore I will boast all the more gladly about my weaknesses, so that Christ's power may rest on me." - 2 **Corinthians 12:7-9 NIV**

Here we see Paul dealing with this thing that he is struggling with, but when he prayed about it, he was told that even in the struggle, the divine power of Christ, or grace, would strongly sustain him. Paul actually makes the connection that in his weakness, he is able to see an all-powerful manner of grace come alive in him, giving him the ability to overcome the issue. Not only does he feel empowered by this grace, he is humbled by it. He sees God's hand at work in his life and he feels more blessed to experience grace in the midst of hardship, than to have the struggle or the "thorn" taken away.

This is the "grace" we felt during that scary time of seizures in our precious daughter. There was a power at work that was not earthly. It was an anointing to endure and preserve us even in such a dark circumstance. There is no doubt in our minds that it had nothing to do with our own strength or power. The grace of God empowers you to do the unthinkable. It enables you to not merely survive, but also, THRIVE in difficulty.

Allow this differing view of grace to impact how you see the surprising and somewhat scary curve balls in your life. Instead of thinking that YOU have to fix everything that seems outside of your power or control, allow God to empower you to live through them. Notice in the account of Paul with his "thorn," we don't read that God removed it for him. We read that God sustained him through GRACE. Furthermore, we read that it is in our moments of "weakness" or rough patches that we can truly experience this grace or divine power. Your troubles are no match for God's grace! There is no hardship that He cannot supernaturally carry you through! Salvation comes through God's favoring grace. But POWER comes through God's supernatural, enabling grace. It is by God's grace we don't harbor fear. It is by God's grace we experience such joy in the midst of grief arising from the thoughts of what we may never experience with our daughter. Most of all, it is by God's grace that we do not allow the unexpected occurrences of this special life to limit us from doing exactly what God has called us to do.

Chapter Five

Truth #3: the Eternity Perspective: Temporary vs. Eternity

While the other two truths discussed in this book are very much critical to remember while dealing with adversity and traversing through the unique roads of special needs, this next truth has to be the easiest one to apply to everyday life IF you believe in a thing called *eternity*. I call this truth the internalizing of the *Eternity Perspective*.

Religions of all kinds have a belief in some kind of eternal life. What happens on the other side of this earthly life is an integral piece of belief systems around the world. In Christianity, we believe that when we accept Christ as our Lord and Savior, when we die, we'll be so privileged to spend the rest of eternity in God's most perfect place of paradise called Heaven. Heaven is described in Revelation 21:4 as a place where "There will be no more crying or pain." 1 Corinthians 15 even says that we'll have "imperishable bodies" in Heaven! Can you imagine trading in your body for a new one that is disease-free and pain-free? Furthermore, what kind of joy does it give you to imagine your child with no more physical, mental or behavioral disability or limitation? What a tremendous thought! If you are like me and you believe that this blissful place is where we will spend countless more days than we will here in this troubled, earthly life, you SHOULD have so much hope. You see, if eternity is an infinite reality, then that also means that the things we face here in this super imperfect world ARE ONLY TEMPORARY! Do you really believe that? When you know something and believe it in the very core of being, your response to situations that may occur in this life is dramatically different. Things have a way of not making you as stressed, crazy or hopeless. You become EMPOWERED.

How does it empower us?

My husband is a "Big Picture" kind of guy. He's not as concerned about what something costs on the front end as much if it is something that will save us money on the back end or in the long run. Honestly, I've learned a lot from him as I've watched him make various kinds of decisions based upon this perspective. When you think about it, much of the most encouraging scriptures in the Bible are "Big Picture" in nature. Here are a few:

• "Weeping endures for a night, but joy comes in the morning." Psalm 30:5 NIV

• "I consider that our present sufferings are not worth comparing with the glory that will be revealed in us." Romans 8:18 NIV

• "The wicked plot against the righteous and gnash their teeth at them; but the Lord laughs a the wicked, for He knows their day is coming." Psalm 37:12-13 NIV

• "You intended to harm me, but God intended it for good to accomplish what is being done now, the saving of many lives." Genesis 50:20 NIV

Now, look at the stories of a few who experienced trials yet overcame. Their accounts of victory are idealized throughout history.

• David, the young, pint-sized, shepherd-boy defeated and prevailed against the threats of a giant.

• Joseph, a boy whose own family disowned him and left him for dead, later held a great place of honor and authority despite the rejection he faced from those closest to him.

• Jesus Christ died. Yet, He rose again just as prophecy said the Messiah would and became the Savior of the World for all of mankind.

Many of us have read these stories countless times! Yet some of us are still ready to accept utter defeat when another bump or undesired moment in life occurs. Read 2 Corinthians 4:17-18 (NIV)

"For our light and momentary troubles are achieving for us an <u>eternal glory</u> that <u>far outweighs them all</u>. So we fix our eyes not on what is <u>seen</u>, but on what is <u>UNSEEN</u>, since what is seen is <u>TEMPORARY</u>, but what is UNSEEN is <u>ETERNAL</u>."

The above scripture says everything I hope you really grasp about Truth #3! If you can see it and are experiencing it, good or bad, it is only temporary. Additionally, you can rest assured it is not a forever thing! If you can rightly distinguish between what is temporary and what is eternal, you equip yourself with the power of truth to fully embrace and love this life. Instead of being focused on something that doesn't matter in the grand scheme of things, you are able to focus on the things that do matter within the scope of eternity. You have a more humbled, yet stable handle on this life in general. Your attitude, decisions, opinions and most importantly, your actions, are all based upon the fact that you know that there is something much greater at work than the momentary thing presenting itself to you.

In the same way that this truth helps you make wiser decisions about things, it also helps you just DEAL better. The fact that our daughter has so many physical limitations and her very life threatened by health issues could be VERY devastating and really is very devastating to many parents in our shoes. When I tell you that this Eternity Perspective, grants me supernatural peace and joy, not to mention, my very sanity, I do not over-exaggerate. She is unable to walk—*now*. She is unable to talk—*now*. She has many physical conditions that we've had to live with day in and day out—*now*. However, what is "unseen" is that she'll have one of those "imperishable bodies" one day…*forever*. There is no *scoliosis* in Heaven's eternity. In fact, there is no disability of any kind. This life is really just a blink in the scope of eternity. We live daily with that understanding. So when the hard moments come, we face them with the color of this truth at work in our heart and minds. Furthermore, her life, in eternal fashion, is really a magnificent one. Her life is used every day to show us the grace and power of God. Through this life of being her parents, we get to experience the remarkably intimate things about God that many people go their whole lives without realizing. How could we ever trade that purpose, just to have a more "normal" way of life? She's truly more of a blessing to us than we could have ever imagined and we praise God every day for showing us the "Big Picture" throughout her life.

What are you facing today, which may only be temporary? What have you allowed yourself to stress and stew over which in the perspective of eternity will not and CANNOT last forever? God and His Kingdom are eternal. Everything else outside of that is only temporary. I challenge you to begin to actually treat the trials that arise in your life, as they are simply temporary. If you treat them as such, your life can noticeably be more peaceful and less of a struggle. In fact, you may find yourself having the energy to not only be a successful parent to your child, but also to fulfill the other things in this life God may call you to!

Chapter Six

LOVING the "SPECIAL" Life

Picture yourself in a traffic jam. You see several cars passing you by and you think "Maybe I should change lanes because that lane will take me further, faster." So you change lanes, and what happens? The new lane now comes to a dead stop and the previous lane you were in is now moving on ahead, leaving you in your feelings of folly. This is quite familiar for many of us when we just don't feel like we're getting as far in life as we were made to travel. Or, maybe you just feel like you're not performing at your greatest. You know you can do better but no matter how hard you try, you fall short. I call this *The Frustration of Mediocrity.*

Mediocrity brings a *"blah"* feeling to life. It is not easy to wholeheartedly love your life when you feel like everything is just "*blah.*" Let's be honest. You love your child, but can you honestly say that you feel a tangible excitement about your life? It was a long time before I could truthfully say that I LOVE MY LIFE! When I realized that there was much more to this life to do in addition to being my daughter's mom, and got busy doing it, my life became more glamorous than I would have ever imagined!

Sometimes we allow the unique circumstances our lives offer limit us from experiencing all we're meant to experience. I am a mom with a child who can't do anything for herself. It would be so easy to use that as an excuse to check out of everything else God may ask of me to do. But God placed things, passions, and abilities inside me to perform in other areas, in addition to being a mommy to this blessing of a child. There are people who need what I have to offer and it would be a disservice to the whole world to withhold those offerings, because I am so focused on the fact that my child is different from most other children. Not only would that be a disservice to the world but also, I myself would feel rather unfulfilled. I would feel something is missing from my life and that I'm just...here. As a consequence of giving in to this state of apathetic mediocrity, there would be obvious resentment over the adversity in my life.

The adversity we may face as a special needs parent is not meant so we can play the victim card. Adversity is opportunity for the greatness within you to rise from the background. Adversity has the potential to bring out the "fight" in you. Troubles may come, but thank God, we do not have to succumb to them. Know who you are in Christ. Know the Truth to which you can hold in your soul and spirit and that empowers you. Operate in God's grace and see the perspective of **His** sovereign timing. If you can live your life this way, there is no reason why you can't be entirely thrilled about your amazing life! Even, against all kinds of troubles, you can absolutely experience the best things in this life to cherish. Jesus did give us this hope-filled wisdom to remember!

"In this world, you will have trouble. But take heart! I have overcome the world!" **John 16:33 NLT**

Paul mentioned in 2 Corinthians 12:9, that he could boast in his weakness because he knew that even in his weakness, God's powerful grace could rise up on his behalf within him. When problems arise, do you feel compelled to solve them? Women are especially known for being problem solvers but many times, it is to our detriment. A problem arises and we put on our Superwoman gear and get to work to control the situation. I know what you may be thinking. "What's wrong with wanting to fix something or make it right?" Here it is. We are not meant to fix everything. And what happens when you work tirelessly to fix something in your own power and no matter how hard you try, you can't fix it?

You become grossly unhappy and feel like a failure. Again, I've been there! Everything that seems problematic doesn't need your fixing. Some things need only for you to submit to the One who is the Ultimate Fixer.

Paul goes on to show us that you can actually still LOVE your life even in all the hard stuff.

*"That is why, for Christ's sake, **I delight** in weaknesses, in insults, in hardships, in persecutions, in difficulties. For when I am weak, then I am strong."* 2 Corinthians 12:10 NIV

How great is that? One of the most persecuted Christians in history, is essentially saying here, "I'm cool with this tough stuff! Through his strength, it's all good!"

Some of us as parents of special needs children are consistently seeing our trials as something that is happening TO us rather than something being used to prove how amazing life can be, even in the midst of difficult moments. When you are able to stop and thank God for the victory over your momentary troubles, you become abundantly more joyful for the big picture of the real blessing your life indeed really is. Your life is different. However, your life was never supposed to be compared to anyone else's to determine what it lacks. It lacks nothing. This is your awesome life. You have things that others don't know what it's like to endure. This actually gives you much more perspective to be thankful for the ultimate strength, peace, and joy only God can give. Understand that this "SPECIAL" life is a spectacular life!

Do you realize the potential you have to absolutely transform someone's life? You can inspire others in ways people with "normal" children cannot! People are watching you. People need to know when things get hard, what they should do, and how they should respond. Your life can provide a helpful example of that. This does not mean that your life will be perfect. It means that people will have a realistic example of how to live with joy in the midst of trials, or during life's scary, uncertain moments.

Learning to embrace and love this life is absolutely an inspiration to others. Moreover, it makes YOU a better special needs mom. When you are loving your life, you are a much healthier person to care for and love your child; and that is definitely worth adopting a more improved perspective. Your joyful heart is more powerful than you can imagine! So here's to you, Mom. May you fully embrace and cherish everything this "SPECIAL" life has to offer and may you one day, help someone else to do the same. Amen.

Index

Identity Scriptures

I am a conqueror - Romans 8:35, 37 NIV

I am strong in Christ's power - Philippians 4:13 NIV

I was made to do great things - Ephesians 2:10 NIV

I have a good calling and future - Jeremiah 29:11 NIV

I need Jesus - John 15:5 NIV

I belong to God and am redeemed by Him - Isaiah 43:1 NIV

I am fearfully and wonderfully made -

Psalm 139:14 NIV

My heart and soul is more to important to God than my external appearance - 1 Samuel 16:7 NIV

I am created by God and protected by Him - Psalm 100:3 NIV

I am a child of God uniquely crafted by His hands - Isaiah 64:8 NIV

I have incredible power given to me by God - Ephesians 1:18-21 NIV

I am a part of the body of Christ - 1 Corinthians 12:27 NIV

I am loved by Jesus who gave His life for me - Galatians 2:20 NIV

Because Christ is in me, I am an overcomer - 1 John 4:4 NIV

I am valuable to God - Matthew 6:26 NIV

As a child of God and co-heir of Christ's I will inherit all promised to me - Romans 8:16-17 NIV

My needs will be met by God - Philippians 4:19 NIV

Because I am His, God will work everything out for my good - Romans 8:28 NIV

About the Author

 Shy and quiet as a child, Rhianna Sanford is now fearless and bold concerning God and His Kingdom. During her adolescent years, she realized God's powerful grace and embraced His call on her life to lead, teach and train people in various areas of ministry. Her ultimate passion, as a formally trained musician, is leading individuals into intimate encounters with God through her musical gifts. During her time as a youth pastor, Rhianna compassionately served teenagers and enlightened them of their power as young people and Christ's co-laborers. This time in youth ministry led her to write *The*

Identity of Purity: A Teenage Girl's Guide to Sexual Purity empowering teenage girls to avoid the common pitfalls in their modern world.

Rhianna and her husband, Alessandro, are uniquely gifted as pioneers and initiators. They founded Living Waters Family Church in Courtland, Kansas and pastored there for 7 years. In Rhianna's more recent years, God has used her as a vessel to inspire others to live at their best from both wellness and spiritual perspectives through writing, blogging and social media. Today, Rhianna is an active, homeschooling mom of three, and entrepreneur living in the Kansas City area. As a busy mother, active choir member at her local church, writer, and wellness educator, Rhianna's sole desire is to do everything God has created her to do, nothing more and nothing less. Her obedience and commitment to serve God's Kingdom is at the root of a life-long theme from Matthew 6:33; to passionately pursue God's ways first and expect the goodness and glory of God to take care of everything else.

Email Rhianna Sanford at letschat@rhiannasanford.com

Find Rhianna on Facebook: facebook.com/rhiannasanford

For more info on Rhianna, go to www.rhiannasanford.com

Made in the USA
Coppell, TX
27 February 2021

50898484R10046